Yasmine Yogi and Phoebe Bee

Dedicated to Jasmine and Phoebe, with love.

Hello I'm Kath. I work in schools and in the community running Relax Kids courses and Yoga classes for children and adults.

During Covid-19 I couldn't do my usual work, so this book was created! I hope you enjoy reading it as much as I loved writing it.

I live with my husband Rob and our 2 girls, Jasmine and Phoebe, in Basingstoke, Hampshire.

Welcome to my book introducing Yasmine Yogi and Phoebe Bee.

DISCLAIMER: This book is intended to be a gentle introduction to yoga for kids. Very gentle yoga postures along with breathing and mindful exercises to bring some peace and calm into your lives. It's great for adults too!

As with any exercise, please listen to your body and don't push your body too far. The exercises in this book should all feel comfortable. If anything doesn't feel comfortable then please stop and perhaps try another time.

This is the first in a series of books designed to help children find their inner peace and calm.

Regular practice of yoga, breathing and mindful exercises have so many benefits and help children to be more aware of how they are feeling.

Hello my name is Phoebe Bee. I am 7 years old and I live with my family (mummy, daddy and my sister Jasmine) in Basingstoke in Hampshire.

I'm a cheeky bee and I am here in this book to teach you some breathing and mindful exercises that you can do to help yourself.

I want to be a ninja bee when I grow up. I love jumping on my trampoline and riding my bike.

Hello I am Yasmine Yogi and I am 10 years old. I live with my mum, dad and sister, Phoebe, in Basingstoke, Hampshire.

My real name is Jasmine, but I thought Yasmine worked better with Yogi. I love reading and maths.

This book is an introduction to the characters, Yasmine Yogi and Phoebe Bee. It is also an introduction to gentle yoga, breathing and mindfulness exercises.

This book has different exercises to help children in those moments that they might find a bit tricky.

Sometimes we might feel angry, sometimes we might feel sad, sometimes we might feel worried or anxious, sometimes we might find it hard to sleep at night.

Please try the yoga exercises that Yasmine Yogi shows you and the breathing and mindful exercises that Phoebe Bee shows you. If you use this book regularly, hopefully you'll start to feel the benefits.

So, let's get started.

Phoebe Bee wants to teach you her most favourite breathing exercise ever. Do you have any idea what it might be?

It is bumblebee breathing. Did you get it right?

To do bumblebee breathing you need to cover your ears, take a deep breath in and as you breathe out make a humming sound. Huuuummmmmm. Does that make your ears feel buzzy?

This is a great breathing exercise to help us feel peaceful and calm. See if you can do this slowly 5 times.

Yasmine Yogi loves to sit peacefully.

Why don't you try this?

Sit comfortably with your legs crossed and your hands on your knees, with a nice straight back.

Close your eyes, breathe in through your nose and breathe out through your nose.

See if you can do this for at least 2 minutes.

Phoebe Bee loves to sit quietly each day and practice her listening.

She thinks it's nice to just listen to the sounds around her. Why not give this a go?

Sit comfortably and maybe close your eyes.

Can you notice any sounds going on around you?

What can you hear?

Yasmine Yogi loves to sit up straight. Sometimes she pretends there is a piece of string running from the ground up through her back to the top of her head, helping her to sit up nice and tall.

Her legs are out nice and straight (but you can bend them if you find that more comfortable) and her hands are by her side.

Spend a moment in this position just breathing in and breathing out. See if you can breathe slowly.

Phoebe Bee loves to count her breath. She uses the numbers 1, 2 and 3.

Start by sitting quietly. We are going to breathe in and count to 1 in our mind, then breathe out and count to 1 in our mind.

Then breathe in and count to 2 in our mind, then breathe out and count to 2 in our mind.

Finally breathe in and count to 3 in our mind, then breathe out and count to 3 in our mind.

Can you do this for 2 minutes?

Yasmine Yogi wants to show you a yoga pose called Butterfly. It's a little bit like the first yoga pose we did in the book, but our legs aren't crossed.

We have the bottoms of our feet touching and we just let our knees relax while we hold on to our feet. This gives us a lovely gentle stretch.

You could try gently moving your legs up and down like butterfly wings, but make sure you do this slowly.

You might want to close your eyes and imagine a beautiful butterfly.

Phoebe Bee wants you to teach you triangle breathing. Do you know what a triangle looks like? A triangle has 3 sides.

Can you see a triangle on this page? With triangle breathing we are going to draw a triangle on our hand, or we can trace around the triangle on this page.

We breathe in as we draw one side, we hold our breath just for 1 second as we draw the second side, and then we breathe out as we finish the triangle.

Can you do that? Now try repeating this exercise for 2 minutes.

Yasmine Yogi is going to show you a yoga pose where you can practice balancing. How still can you be?

Can you copy her? If you need to hold on to something as you try this one that's fine, sometimes it takes a little practice. Do this on both sides. (Please make sure you don't rest your foot on your knee.)

Is one side easier than the other?

Phoebe Bee wants you to give yourself a big hug! She wants to tell you how to do butterfly taps.

Start off stretching your arms out wide and then bring them back to give yourself a big hug. You can try butterfly taps up and down your back.

Just like little rain drops as you tap, tap, tap up and down your back.

Please don't overstretch though. This should feel nice and comfortable.

Yasmine Yogi loves to stretch.

Standing with your legs nice and straight, lift one arm up towards the ceiling or the sky and slowly and gently reach over to the other side.

Just a gentle stretch though, don't overdo it.

Once you've stretched over to one side, do exactly the same on the other side. Enjoy a lovely stretch.

Phoebe Bee wants you to take a look around the space you are in and to notice different colours. Maybe point at those colours or say what you are looking at quietly in your mind.

Can you see something red?
Can you see something orange?
Can you see something yellow?
Can you see something green?
Can you see something blue?
Can you see something purple?

Yasmine Yogi loves to stretch her body out from top to toe. Please make sure you stretch comfortably though. We don't want to hurt ourselves.

We start with our legs stretched out wide and then we stretch our arms out wide. Then see how big we can make our smile!

And while we are doing this, we can practice taking a deep breath in and breathing out slowly.

Phoebe Bee sometimes finds it tricky to go to sleep, so she practices counting her out breath. She starts at 20 and counts backwards. Can you count backwards?

Phoebe Bee takes a deep breath in and as she breaths out she says in her mind 20. Then another breath in and, as she breathes out, she says in her mind 19. Another slow breath in and, as she breathes out, she says in her mind 18, then 17, 16, 15 and all the way back to 1.

If she's still awake when she gets to 1, she starts it again. Why not give this one a try at bedtime?

Yasmine Yogi wants to teach you a yoga posture called downward facing dog.

Yasmine Yogi thinks it looks more like a triangle shape. What do you think? Can you do this one? Start off on your hands and knees with a nice flat back and then push your bottom up into the air and feel a very gentle stretch down your back and down your legs. Stay here for a few moments practicing your breathing.

Phoebe Bee wants to teach you a calming breathing exercise. She loves to practice this one when she is feeling a bit sad.

Start by making yourself comfortable, and then close your eyes. Imagine you are sat outside on a lovely sunny day. Imagine there are lots of fluffy white clouds in the sky.

Now you are going to imagine you are sending any sad thoughts to the clouds. Then take a big breath in and imagine you are blowing those clouds away. Try again.

Breathe in and as you breathe out, pretend you are blowing the clouds away and your sad thoughts are blowing away with the clouds.

Yasmine Yogi loves to curl up into a little ball like a hedgehog when she's had a day that hasn't gone so well. She goes onto her knees and puts her forehead on the floor with her arms stretched out in front of her.

Why don't you try? While you're curled up notice your breathing. Really notice your in breath and your out breath.

Phoebe Bee loves to say positive words about herself. Her favourite word is 'amazing' and she often says to herself 'I am amazing'. That makes her feel a little bit amazing.

Can you think of a positive word to describe yourself and can you say it out loud?

Here are some ideas for you:

I am amazing
I am brave
I am calm
I am kind
I am loved
I am special

Yasmine Yogi loves to play around in this position before she relaxes! This is called happy baby pose.

Lie down on your back with your hands and feet in the air with your knees bent. When you are ready see if you can reach your toes (keeping your knees soft). Stay in this position for a moment, just gently rocking from side to side.

Phoebe Bee wants to teach you a breathing exercise she likes to do at bedtime.

It's called tummy breathing. Tummy breathing is super easy. All you need to do is lie down on your back and pop your hands on your tummy. See if you can notice your tummy rising and falling as you breathe in and breathe out.

Just notice your tummy rising and falling as you breathe in and breathe out.

You might have a small soft toy that you can pop on your tummy and see if you can make it go up and down on your tummy.

Yasmine Yogi thinks you've worked really hard, and she thinks it's time for a rest.

So if you lie down and close your eyes. Start to notice your breathing. Breathe in and breathe out, breathe in and breathe out while you listen to the short relaxation on the next page.

RELAXATION WITH PHOEBE BEE

Close your eyes and become as still as possible. Pop your hands on your tummy and see if you can notice your tummy rising and falling as you breathe in and breathe out. Just notice your tummy rising and falling as you breathe in and breathe out.

Just spend some time enjoying some peace and calm after you've worked hard today.

Now can you relax each part of your body in turn? Relax your toes, relax your feet, relax your legs, relax your tummy, relax your lower back, relax your upper back, relax your chest, relax your arms, relax your hands, relax your fingers, relax your head. Be super still and lie there for a moment feeling very, very relaxed.

Now put your hands on your heart. Notice your heart. Can you feel your heart beating?

Just take a moment to notice. Now feel all the love in your heart. Just take a moment to feel the love in your heart.

What does that love feel like?

Now, think of someone you love very much. See a picture of that person in your mind. Imagine that you are sending some love to that person.

Just imagine the love going from your heart to their heart. How happy does that make you feel? How happy does that make them feel? Enjoy sending love from your heart to the heart of someone you love very much.

I hope you enjoyed this book. Please keep an eye out for more books which I'll be putting on my website (www.kazaar.co.uk).

For more information on my classes and courses – in schools, in the community and online – please check out my website www.relaxwithkath.com

Written by Kath Routledge
Illustrations (Yasmine Yogi and Phoebe Bee) by Md Ferdin Kamal Nerob
Other Illustrations from Daily Art Hub (www.dailyarthub.com)

Printed in Poland
by Amazon Fulfillment
Poland Sp. z o.o., Wrocław